BY V.C. THOMPSON

CONSPIRACY THEORIES DEBUNKED

THE SIMPSONS PREDICT THE FUTURE

Published in the United States of America by Cherry Lake Publishing

Ann Arbor, Michigan

www.cherrylakepublishing.com

Editorial Consultant: Dr. Virginia Loh-Hagan, EdD, Literacy, San Diego State University

Reading Adviser: Beth Walker Gambro, MS, Ed., Reading Consultant, Yorkville, IL

Photo Credits: © Jessica Rogner, cover, 1, interior graphics; Public Domain/Wikimedia, 4; © DC Studio/Shutterstock, 7; © Gavrilo Stanojevic/Shutterstock, 9; © Bill Oakley/Wikimedia, 11; © insta_photos/Shutterstock, 13; © David Pereiras/Shutterstock, 14; © Giovanni Cancemi/Shutterstock, 17; © Vitaliken/Shutterstock, 19; © Joseph Sohm/Shutterstock, 21; © Autopilot/Wikimedia, 22; © Debby Wong/Shutterstock, 25; © Rena Schild/Shutterstock, 26

45th Parallel Press is an imprint of Cherry Lake Publishing Group.

Library of Congress Cataloging-in-Publication Data has been filed and is available at catalog.loc.gov

ABOUT THE AUTHOR

V. C. Thompson is a nurse and author living in Michigan. V. C. is husband to his lovely wife, Anna. Together they are the proud parents of two children, one in Heaven and one newborn. His mission in life is to share his faith through the written word and the healing hand.

TABLE OF CONTENTS

There are many unsolved mysteries. The Voynich Manuscript is one. It is a 600-year-old book written in a language no one knows!

INTRODUCTION

The world is filled with mysteries. Mysteries are things or events that cannot be easily explained. Some mysteries are conspiracies. Conspiracies are secret plans made by a group of people. Most conspiracies are stories that have no evidence. Evidence is proof. It is facts or information that supports a claim. Some conspiracies are later found out to be true. But most conspiracies are false. Sometimes it is hard to tell which conspiracies are true and which are false.

People who believe in conspiracies are called conspiracy theorists. Theorists are people who explain things with ideas called theories. Most people think conspiracy theorists are wrong. Some conspiracy theories are easy to prove wrong. Others are harder to prove wrong. Some are funny. Others are very serious.

Some people call conspiracy theorists crazy or stupid. This is hurtful. It is wrong to attack people, even if what they think is incorrect. Instead, the conspiracy theory should be examined. To examine a conspiracy theory, look at the evidence. Almost every claim has evidence. What matters is *how much* evidence there is and how strong it is. This tells us if the theory is true or false.

Let's take a look at a popular conspiracy theory. Don't forget to keep track of all the evidence. At the end, see if you can debunk this conspiracy yourself!

In rare cases, some conspiracies turned out to be true. Many believed the U.S. government was experimenting on mind control. And they were. MK-ULTRA was a top secret program. It was led by the CIA.

CHAPTER 1:

THE PREMISE

The Simpsons is an adult cartoon. The show has been on television since 1989. The show has been running for more than 30 years. More than 700 episodes have been made. Different people write these episodes. There have been nearly 140 writers over the years.

Each episode is very funny. The main character, Homer Simpson, is married to Marge Simpson. They are the parents of Bart, Lisa, and Maggie Simpson. They live in a town called Springfield. The Simpsons are always getting themselves into trouble.

Some of the other characters are based on people in real life. Some of the places in the show are real places. Even some of the events in the show really happened.

The show makes fun of these people, places, and events. This makes the show part fiction and part nonfiction. Fiction means not true. Nonfiction stories are true.

A conspiracy theory about the show claims *The Simpsons* predicts the future. To predict is to guess what will happen. There are many examples of this. Some scenes seem so close to what happened in real life.

The Simpsons often uses satire. Satire is a type of writing method. It uses humor to prove a point.

SPOT-LIGHT

BRAINIACS

The people behind *The Simpsons* are really smart. *The Simpsons* producer Al Jean is a great example. He studied math at Harvard University at 16 years old! One of the writers, Jeff Westbrook, attended Princeton University and Harvard University. He even taught about computers at Yale University. These colleges are among the best in the world. They're all difficult to get admitted to. A conspiracy theorist might say this proves the show staff are evil geniuses!

Some conspiracy theorists say this cannot be a coincidence. A coincidence is when situations happen at the same time without planning. But these scenes were aired before the real events! The conspiracy theorists say *The Simpsons* writers know the future. There is a great deal of evidence for this conspiracy. Let's examine it further.

The Simpsons writers wrote about events before they happened in real life. Do you think it's all a coincidence? Pictured are some of the show's writers.

CHAPTER 2:

TECHNOLOGY

CONSPIRACY

In 1995, *The Simpsons* predicted video chatting. Lisa called Marge over a rotary phone. Rotary phones are large telephones with a dial wheel. In the show, the rotary phone had a screen. Lisa used this phone to video chat with Marge. Video chat is when phones use cameras during the call. An example of video chatting would be FaceTiming or Zoom meetings. This technology seems advanced for 1995!

The same happened with smartwatches. Smartwatches are computer watches. In the same episode, another character talks into his watch. The watch had buttons and a screen and even made noises. Smartwatches became popular 19 years later. How could someone predict that?

Zoom was founded in 2011. But it didn't become common and widespread until the COVID-19 pandemic in 2020.

The first modern smartwatch was invented by Steve Mann.

DEBUNKED

Did *The Simpsons* really predict video chat and smartwatches? Well, probably not. Video chat was actually invented in 1964 by the telephone company AT&T. It was called Picturephone. *The Simpsons* showed this technology before it was popular. For most people, it seemed new. It wasn't popular until the early 2000s. So it was not a prediction after all.

The same is true of smartwatches. People had been talking about the idea since the 1950s. Many movies, shows, and comic books featured smartwatches. In fact, basic smartwatches were invented in 1994. This was a year before *The Simpsons* episode aired. The show just showed the technology before it was popular.

CHAPTER 3:

EBOLA VIRUS

THE CONSPIRACY

A deadly sickness spread in Africa in 2014. This sickness was called the Ebola virus. A virus is a germ that infects people. The Ebola virus killed many people. *The Simpsons* predicted this virus in 1997. That is 14 years before the outbreak! In the episode, Marge picks up a book. The book is called *Curious George and the Ebola Virus*. How did the show's writers predict this virus?

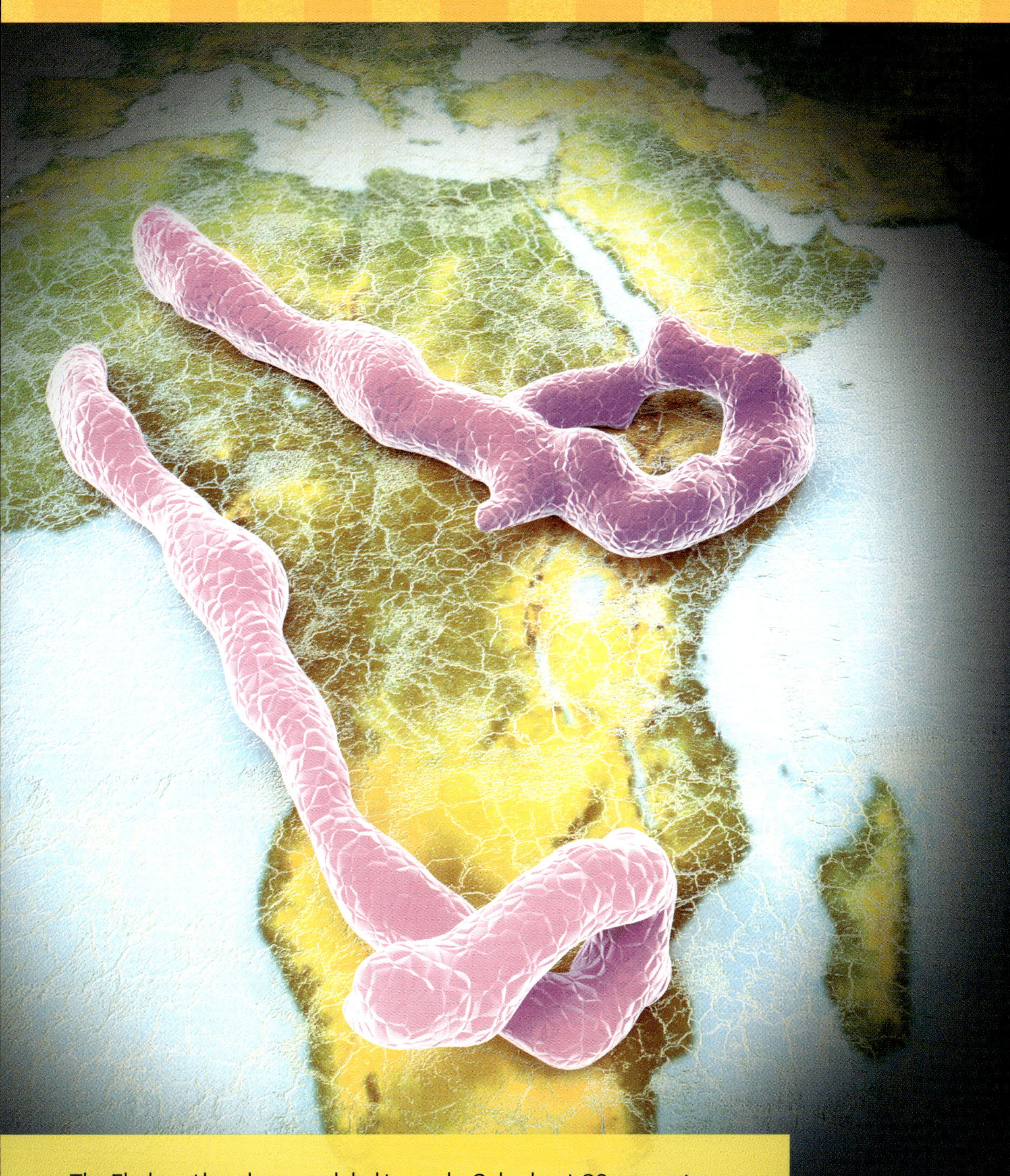

The Ebola outbreak was a global tragedy. Only about 60 percent of those infected survived.

SPOT-LIGHT

OPTICAL ILLUSIONS

The brain works in amazing ways. Sometimes our brains can mislead us. Optical illusions are examples of this. Another example is bias. Bias is when your feelings stop you from being fair. One type of bias is confirmation bias. This is when you force new evidence to agree with your views. Here's an example. Aaron believes *The Simpsons* conspiracy. He thinks the show predicted COVID-19. He will watch each episode looking for clues. When he sees Homer with a cough, he will say this is proof. In reality, Homer only had a cold. Aaron's brain tricked him. He was only looking for what he wanted to see. Aaron was forcing the evidence to agree with his theory.

DEBUNKED

It seems *The Simpsons* predicted the Ebola virus outbreak. Except it didn't predict an outbreak. It only showed the character Curious George getting Ebola. The Ebola virus was actually discovered in 1976. Two scientists named Guido van der Groen and Peter Piot discovered it. *The Simpsons* creators picked a virus people didn't know. It was only a coincidence that an outbreak happened years later.

CHAPTER 4:

9/11

THE CONSPIRACY

In 2001, America was attacked by terrorists. Terrorists are people who use violence and threats to get what they want. The terrorists flew planes into the World Trade Center's Twin Towers. These 2 famous buildings were in New York City. The terrorist attack killed almost 3,000 people. This attack is called 9/11 because it happened on September 11.

A 1997 episode of *The Simpsons* predicted this! In the episode, Lisa holds up a New York bus tour pamphlet. Pictured is $9 and the Twin Towers. The $9 lines up with the Twin Towers on the cover. This spells 9/11. Was this a prediction?

The Simpsons has been called the "animated Nostradamus." Nostradamus was a French astrologer. He was known for his predictions. He lived in the 1500s.

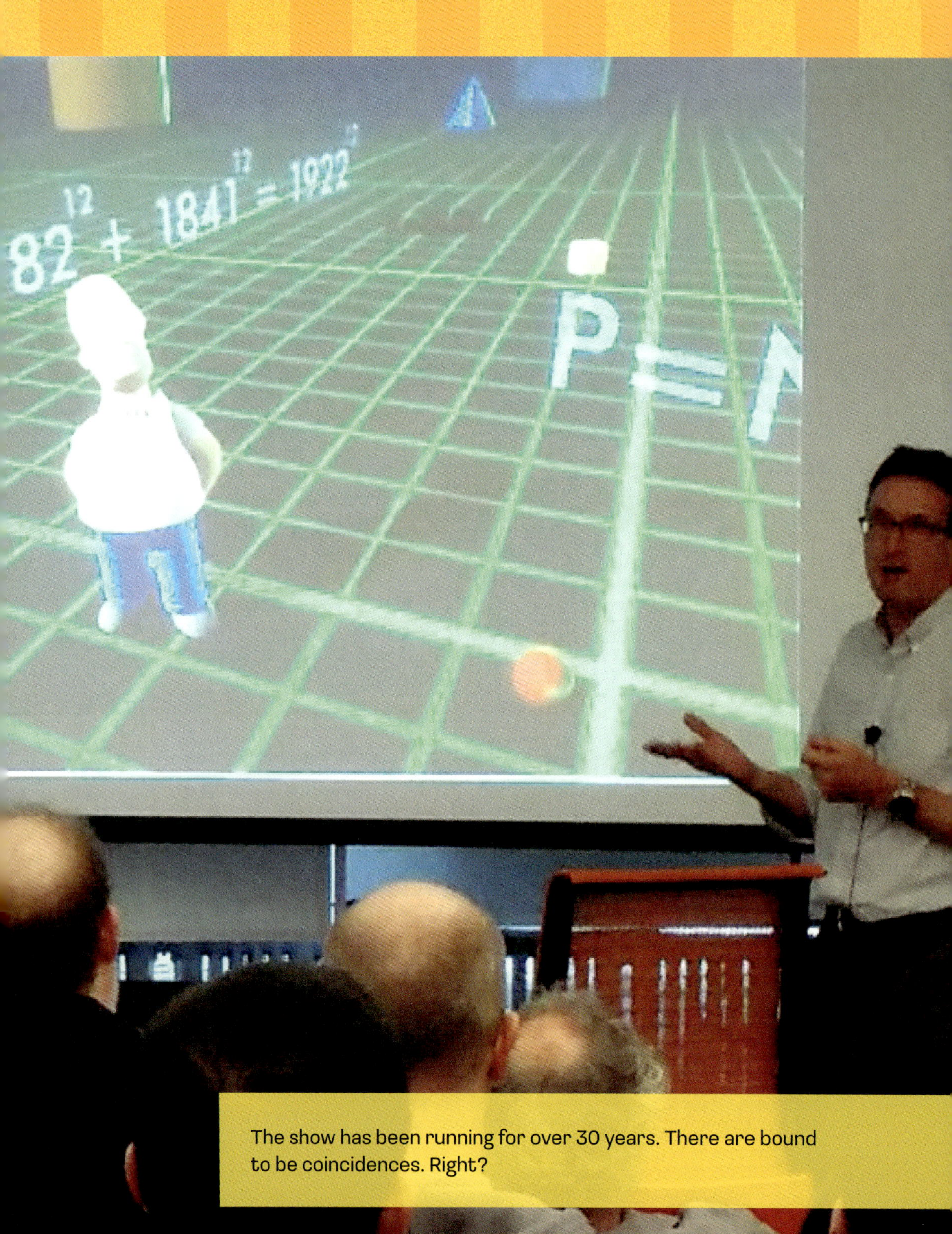

The show has been running for over 30 years. There are bound to be coincidences. Right?

DEBUNKED

The 9/11 prediction is a strange one. This scene really did happen before 9/11. So was it a true prediction? It's eerie but not a true prediction.

The pamphlet Lisa holds up was supposed to be funny. New York bus tours are expensive, even in 1997! The price of $9 is extremely cheap. The writers picked the price to be funny. And the Twin Towers were famous. The buildings were part of the city's skyline.

It is just a coincidence that the attack happened on 9/11. *The Simpsons* writers deny that they knew about the attack. Co-creator Al Jean said, "If you throw enough darts, you're going to get some bullseyes." He meant that if someone makes a lot of guesses, some of them will likely come true.

CHAPTER 5:

DONALD TRUMP

THE CONSPIRACY

Did you know *The Simpsons* predicted Trump's presidency? Donald Trump was elected president in 2016. Before that, he was a well-known business owner. Nobody thought he would be president. Nobody except *The Simpsons*!

In a 2000 episode, the show predicted that Trump would run for president. The episode showed him waving on an escalator. This scene came true in 2015! Even the details are the same. Someone dropped a Trump sign in the scene. The same happened in real life. Trump waved with his right hand. That happened in real life. Trump gave a thumbs-up with his left hand. That also happened in real life.

Before becoming president, Donald Trump (center) was famous for *The Apprentice*. It was a reality television show.

The writers didn't actually think Donald Trump would become president!

DEBUNKED

How could the President Trump prediction *not* be real? Well, it is a real prediction! But it was only a joke. Donald Trump was very famous. This is why *The Simpsons* creators picked him. It is also part of why he became president. *The Simpsons* writer Dan Greaney explains it best: "*The Simpsons* has always kind of embraced the over-the-top side of American culture . . . and [Trump] is just the fulfillment of that." In short, Trump was over-the-top. At the time, this was funny. *The Simpsons* show is over-the-top and funny. So *The Simpsons* featured Trump.

What about the escalator scene? That scene was made *after* Trump became president. The video short is called *Trumptastic Voyage*. It was released in 2015. It went viral. People claimed it was from the original episode. It wasn't.

SPOT-

EXAGGERATED TRUTH

Many conspiracy theories sound true. They sound like they're based on facts. Often, these theories do have some truth to them. But sometimes it's truth that has been exaggerated. Exaggerated truth can be harmless. You might say, "I have a million things to do today! I don't have time to clean my room." This is a harmless exaggeration. But sometimes exaggerated truth can cause harm. Sometimes the media does this. They exaggerate negative news.

One way to deal with this is to research. Research means digging deeper into a topic. Investigate questions. Find and organize information from several sources. Read books on the topic. Talk to experts. Talk to eyewitnesses. Use research to fact-check theories.

LIGHT

CHAPTER 6:

THE VERDICT

The Simpsons conspiracy theory is very interesting. What other show makes prophecies like this? Prophecies are predictions that come true. Are the writers prophets? Do people in real life copy the show? Is it just plain luck?

Some scenes are easy to explain. The show has a lot of episodes. Every episode has predictions. With so many predictions, some are bound to come true. That is evidence against the conspiracy.

Behind every conspiracy, there is a motive to keep the secret. A motive is a reason to do something. Let's say the show's writers can really see the future. What motive is there for hiding their ability? There doesn't seem to be a good one. That is more evidence against the conspiracy theory.

This is conspiracy theory has been DEBUNKED. Or has it? What do you think?

TRY THIS!

1. Write down 3 predictions for next week. Make the predictions possible but unlikely. Did any of them come true?

2. Study famous prophecies. Famous astrologer Nostradamus made many. Did any of these prophesies come true?

3. Listen for people making predictions. News stations do this every day. Watch to see if any of their predictions come true.

4. Watch an episode of your favorite television show. Look for any predictions. Then see if they come true.

5. Think about a theory that interests you. Go to the library and find books on it. Evaluate the evidence for and against the theory.

LEARN MORE

Goldstein, Margaret J. *What Are Conspiracy Theories?* Minneapolis, MN: Lerner Publications, 2020.

Johnson, Anna Maria. *Debunking Conspiracy Theories.* New York, NY: Cavendish Square Publishing, LLC, 2019.

GLOSSARY

bias (BY-uhs) favoring one idea because of personal preference

confirmation bias (kahn-fuhr-MAY-shuhn BYE-uhs) noticing only information that supports one's view

conspiracies (kuhn-SPIHR-uh-seez) secret plans to do something bad or against the law

evidence (EH-vuh-duhnss) facts or information that support a claim

fiction (FIK-shuhn) a made-up story

motive (MOH-tiv) a reason to do something

mysteries (MIH-stuh-reez) things that are unknown or hard to explain

nonfiction (nahn-FIK-shuhn) a true story

predicts (PRUH-dikts) guesses what will happen

prophecies (prah-FUH-seez) predictions that come true

research (REE-suhrch) investigating questions by finding and organizing information

rotary phone (ROH-tuh-ree FOHN) large telephones with a dial wheel used until the 1980s

terrorists (TEHR-uhr-ists) people who use violence and threats to get what they want

theorists (THEE-uh-rists) people who explain things with ideas called theories

virus (VYE-ruhs) a germ that infects people

INDEX